HENRY B.

GONZALEZ

CONGRESSMAN OF THE PEOPLE

SPECIAL LIVES IN HISTORY THAT BECOME

Signature LIVES

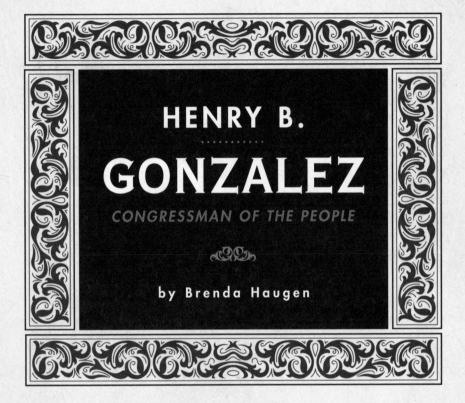

HENRY B.
GONZALEZ

CONGRESSMAN OF THE PEOPLE

by Brenda Haugen

Content Adviser: Armando Cantú Alonzo, Ph.D.,
Associate Professor, Department of History,
Texas A&M University

Reading Adviser: Rosemary G. Palmer, Ph.D.,
Department of Literacy, College of Education,
Boise State University

COMPASS POINT BOOKS  MINNEAPOLIS, MINNESOTA

Compass Point Books
3109 West 50th Street, #115
Minneapolis, MN 55410

Visit Compass Point Books on the Internet at *www.compasspointbooks.com*
or e-mail your request to *custserv@compasspointbooks.com*

Editor: Nick Healy
Lead Designer: Jaime Martens
Photo Researcher: Svetlana Zhurkin
Page Production: Bobbie Nuytten
Cartographer: XNR Productions, Inc.

Managing Editor: Catherine Neitge
Creative Director: Keith Griffin
Editorial Director: Carol Jones

To Jill and Jerry McCord, for always being there for me
and the rest of our family. BLH

The Gonzalez family, Gail Beagle, Henry B. Gonzalez's former chief of
staff, and Heather Trent of The Center for American History at the
University of Texas at Austin provided valuable assistance with this project.

Library of Congress Cataloging-in-Publication Data
Haugen, Brenda.
 Henry B. Gonzalez : congressman of the people / by Brenda Haugen.
  p. cm.—(Signature lives)
 Includes bibliographical references and index.
 ISBN-13: 978-0-7565-0996-5 (hardcover)
 ISBN-10: 0-7565-0996-3 (hardcover)
 ISBN-13: 978-0-7565-1858-5 (paperback)
 ISBN-10: 0-7565-1858-X (paperback)
 1. Gonzalez, Henry B. (Henry Barbosa), 1916—2000 2. Legislators—
United States—Biography. 3. United States. Congress. House—Biography.
4. United States—Politics and government—1945–1989. 5. United
States—Politics and government—1989- 6. Mexican Americans—
Biography. 7. Minorities—Civil rights—United States—History—20th
century. 8. Poor—Civil rights—United States—History—20th century. 9.
Legislators—Texas—Biography. 10. Texas—Politics and government—
1951- I. Title. II. Series.
 E840.8.G63H38 2006
 328.73'092—dc22   2005014461

Signature Lives

MODERN AMERICA

Starting in the late 19th century, advancements in all areas of human activity transformed an old world into a new and modern place. Inventions prompted rapid shifts in lifestyle, and scientific discoveries began to alter the way humanity viewed itself. Beginning with World War I, warfare took place on a global scale, and ideas such as nationalism and communism showed that countries were taking a larger view of their place in the world. The combination of all these changes continues to produce what we know as the modern world.

Henry B. Gonzalez

Table of Contents

1 A VOICE THAT ENDURED

Chapter

ᕦᕤ

Henry B. Gonzalez's throat burned, and his body ached with exhaustion. Yet he knew he must continue speaking. People throughout the state of Texas were depending on him.

Senator Abraham "Chick" Kazen, a fellow Democrat, had started the filibuster in an attempt to defeat bills designed to uphold segregation throughout Texas. He talked late into the night before giving the floor to Gonzalez. Dressed in his favorite powder blue suit, a yellow tie with matching handkerchief, and bright white shoes, Gonzalez now stood determined before the rest of the Texas Senate.

"I seek to register the plaintive cry, the hurt feelings, the silent, the dumb protest of the inarticulate," he said that evening in May 1957.

Henry B. Gonzalez became the first Mexican-American to serve in the state Senate since Texas' earliest days of statehood.

Gonzalez (left) and Senator Chick Kazen teamed to stop an effort to keep Texas schools and other aspects of life segregated.

He spoke all night, through the next day, and into the second night. With no break to rest, use the bathroom, or eat, Gonzalez talked for 22 hours and two minutes. He sucked on lemons and raisins to help soothe his sore throat.

Finally, Gonzalez could stop talking. When the Senate votes were taken, eight of 10 bills in a package intended to maintain segregation in Texas were defeated. Of the two that passed, one was declared unconstitutional by a federal court.

Gonzalez's filibuster proved to be the longest in Texas history. He wound up not only winning his battle against segregation, but also demonstrating to others how much he knew about the topic. Few people could speak clearly and knowledgeably on a subject

> *A filibuster is a tactic used by lawmakers when they are convinced they must stop a bill's progress but believe they have no other way to defeat it. In a filibuster, a legislator makes a long speech and refuses to stop speaking, which prevents a vote from being taken.*

for nearly a full day. And throughout the entire time, Gonzalez talked without the help of notes.

The Senate filibuster gained national attention for Gonzalez and helped lead him to a career in Congress that would stretch for nearly four decades. But while his job may have become higher profile, Gonzalez stayed the same. From the start of his political career, he worked to make life better for the poor and downtrodden, and his focus never wavered—even when his life was threatened.

Born in 1916, Gonzalez grew up in an area of San Antonio, Texas, populated by the less fortunate. His parents had lived a life of privilege in Mexico until a bloody revolution in the early 1900s forced them to flee north to the United States. They came to the

Gonzalez holds a stack of telegrams praising his stand against segregation in Texas.

United States as refugees, with little more than the clothes on their backs.

Though Gonzalez's family lived more comfortably than most refugees, he and other Mexican-Americans still faced the same sort of discrimination endured by blacks in the South. As a child,

Gonzalez had not been able to swim in the city pool, where white children splashed and played on hot San Antonio afternoons. In many communities, Mexican-Americans couldn't use the same drinking fountains, eat in the same restaurants, or live in the same neighborhoods as whites. Hate groups such as the Ku Klux Klan sometimes terrorized the Mexican-Americans.

As an adult, Gonzalez was determined to change things. And he did. He opened doors to places where Mexican-Americans were never before allowed to go.

He fought against discrimination and for better education and housing for the homeless. He battled to end segregation and supported human rights, fair wages, and honesty in government. He raised a stir when others told him to be quiet. And he worked fearlessly for the rights of all Americans, regardless of the color of their skin or the size of their bank accounts.

Gonzalez also served as a trailblazer, showing other Mexican-Americans they, too, could have a voice in politics. He became the first Mexican-

The Ku Klux Klan formed in the late 1860s after the end of the Civil War. It was started by former Confederate soldiers and quickly grew into an organization that terrorized blacks. Klan groups still exist in the United States today. They believe that whites are superior to other races, and they oppose equal rights for blacks and other minority groups. The Klan continues to use violence and intimidation to promote its beliefs.

American elected to the San Antonio City Council and, later, the first Mexican-American elected from Texas to the U.S. Congress.

Wherever he went, Gonzalez faced discrimination. He was sometimes referred to as "that Mexican" by white colleagues in the halls of government. His opponents tried to dismiss or ignore him, but Gonzalez would not be denied an equal voice as an American. He worked hard to make sure all

Gonzalez is interviewed by a San Antonio television crew during his early years as a congressman.

people were treated fairly. He fought for civil rights, affordable housing, and help for small businesses. And Gonzalez's voice always rang out loudly and clearly regardless of criticism. He took on anyone who disagreed with him, including presidents and other powerful officials.

Though he often found great opposition to his views, Gonzalez discovered that hard work, courage, and honesty gained him respect. Not everyone liked him, but they did respect him.

Gonzalez's long career in Congress brought him into contact with eight presidents.

He lives on through the work he did as a congressman. Today many Americans lead better lives than might have been possible without Henry Gonzalez. They enjoy freedoms and opportunities—the full benefits of being American—because one man from Texas fought tirelessly and refused to be silenced. ✑

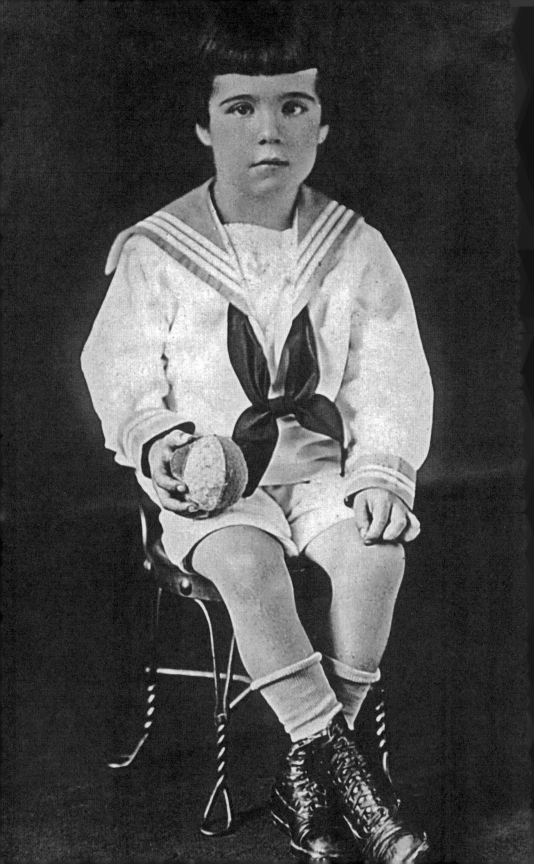

2 SON OF REFUGEES

Henry's face conveyed shock. His second-grade teacher had just told him he was an American. He later said:

> *My wonderful inspiring teacher, Miss Mason, made it clear that if we were born in the United States we were Americans. This was astonishing news, because at home we were being brought up as Mexicans who would eventually go back to the homeland. That evening at the supper table I announced this startling revelation: I am an American because I was born here. But my (aunt) harrumphed: "Well, if that's so, if a cat is born in an oven does that make him bread?" And with that, and the instant laughter and jeers of the crowd of cousins who had just*

Henry Gonzalez as a child in San Antonio, Texas

come from Mexico, I was laughed out of the room: "Ha, ha, he wants to make believe he is a gringo."

Henry's parents, Leonides and Genoveva Gonzalez, came to Texas as refugees, but they always planned to go back to Mexico when the civil war ended and political conditions returned to normal. The 1910 Mexican Revolution had turned the world upside down for the Gonzalez family and others. To escape violence, thousands of Mexicans fled to the United States. Leonides and Genoveva Gonzalez were among them.

They had lived a comfortable life in Mapimí, a city in northern Mexico where Leonides owned and operated silver mines and served as mayor. He also worked for President Porfirio Diaz, who had risen from poverty to become Mexico's ruler. Diaz picked people to fill significant government jobs on all levels, from top federal positions down to local jobs. He selected Leonides to serve in a position that made him the watchdog of other officials in the area.

Diaz's policies had made a few people very rich. However, many people suffered under his rule. Families were forced off their land, and laborers went without work. Tired of seeing the rich get richer, Mexicans staged a violent revolution to overthrow Diaz. A bloody civil war ensued, lasting about a decade. During the war, more than a million

A revolution ended the rule of Mexican President Porfirio Diaz in 1911.

people died, and many homes were destroyed.

When the revolution first erupted, the Gonzalezes had remained in their Mexican home, and Leonides continued to work. However, in early 1911, gangs of revolutionaries and thieves traveled around the country, terrorizing Mexican communities. One group took over Mapimí and captured Leonides.

19

Because he had worked for Diaz, Leonides faced execution at the group's hands. But his life was saved by a good deed he'd done earlier. Juana Lopez, the wife of a local merchant, had not forgotten that before the revolution Leonides had saved her husband and son. The two had been arrested and charged with a serious crime—one that carried the death penalty. Leonides knew the two men were innocent. Other local officials and military leaders wanted the men dead, but he freed them.

Refugees who fled war in Mexico gathered at Fort Bliss in Texas.

Now he needed help, and Juana stood ready. She gathered a band of men and demanded that he be released. Leonides promised his captors they could

have all of his possessions and said he would leave Mexico. The men set him free.

Leonides quickly sent a message to Genoveva to gather their sons, Leonides and Carlos, and other members of their household and to meet him in Monterrey, Mexico. Genoveva hid money and jewels in her clothes, but everything else had to be left behind. From Monterrey, the family traveled by train to Laredo, Texas. They decided to continue on to San Antonio, Texas, where they settled in February 1911.

> *In 1917, Mexico had a new constitution, which allowed for democratic elections. Changes, including shifts in land ownership, were made to help the poor. Despite the revolution and the changes that followed, many Mexicans continued to live in poverty.*

The Gonzalezes lived in a hotel until they ran out of money. Henry's father took whatever jobs he could find to feed and house his family. At one point, they lived in a shack with dirt floors and no running water.

In time, Leonides' situation improved. He began working at *La Prensa*, the only Spanish-language newspaper published daily in San Antonio. Eventually, he became the managing editor, and the family moved into a nicer home on Prospect Hill.

The Gonzalezes spoke no English, and they raised their children to speak Spanish, too. Leonides expected to move his family back to Mexico once the revolution ended. However, that was not to be. Leonides and Genoveva would live in Texas for the rest of their lives.

The Gonzalez family grew during their early years in the United States. In time, Leonides and Genoveva had four more children. The family included five sons and one daughter. Among them was Enrique Barbosa Gonzalez. He would be known as Henry, the English version of his given name. Henry was born May 3, 1916.

A horse-drawn wagon rolls through a San Antonio street in the early 1910s.

By then, the Gonzalez family was living in a modest house in a Mexican neighborhood. Some of their neighbors were very poor and uneducated, but others were more fortunate. Regardless of their financial

situation, the Mexicans were treated like second-class citizens. They faced discrimination in the South similar to what African-Americans faced. They couldn't eat in certain restaurants, attend certain schools, or go swimming in many public pools.

Hate groups also inspired fear. Members of the Ku Klux Klan (KKK) often rode through the Mexican neighborhoods in the middle of the night. Dressed in bed sheets and hoods that hid their identities, the Klansmen threatened the Mexicans. The KKK hated Mexican-Americans not only because they weren't white, but also because many of them—including the Gonzalezes—were Roman Catholics.

When Henry entered first grade, he encountered another problem. He'd been raised to speak Spanish, but only English was spoken at school. In fact, students were punished if they spoke Spanish in the building. Henry later remembered:

> *Fear seemed pervasive, hanging as a heavy fog all around my childhood world. The fear of abject poverty, of dread diseases like tuberculosis, and the fear linked to a hostile, alien neighborhood, speaking with a harsh and unfriendly-sounding, incomprehensible language. There was the terror of being dragged to that first day of school—to its forbidding-looking strange adults and unknown classmates. Not knowing English, I was compelled to spend a whole year in "low first" grade.*

Luckily, most of Henry's teachers understood the difficulties he and many of his classmates faced and were willing to help. Once he overcame the language barrier, Henry excelled in school.

He also found hope in a prayer he read again and again. Written in Spanish, the prayer said, *"Nada te espante,"* or "fear not." The prayer also said to have patience and to be faithful that all would turn out well if one was committed in his or her belief.

> *Henry's middle name, Barbosa, was his mother's maiden name. As he grew older, people called him Henry B., a nickname that would stick with him his whole life.*

"Those words gave me the courage that was essential to self-respect," Henry said. "From then on, fear did not overwhelm me."

While he found it difficult to speak English at first, Henry learned more quickly how to read it. He found refuge in the many books in his local library. From the time he turned 8, Henry became a regular reader of poetry, biographies, novels, and anything else that sparked his interest.

By the time Henry entered junior high, he knew English well, but he spoke with a heavy accent. Because some of his classmates teased him, Henry tried to figure out a way to lose his accent. He found his answer in a book.

One of the characters became a great orator, or

Henry B. Gonzalez's parents, Leonides and Genoveva Gonzalez

public speaker, by practicing his speech with his mouth full of pebbles. Henry thought it was worth a shot.

He tried it at home "until Papa thought I was nuts and told me to stop," Henry later remembered.

So he came up with a plan that didn't involve pebbles. He read aloud while a friend corrected his accent. Then he practiced by watching himself in a mirror as he spoke.

His behavior greatly entertained his sister, who could not contain her snickers. But Henry was determined to speak clearly and to lose his accent. Little did he know that he would someday become known for his exceptional speaking skills.

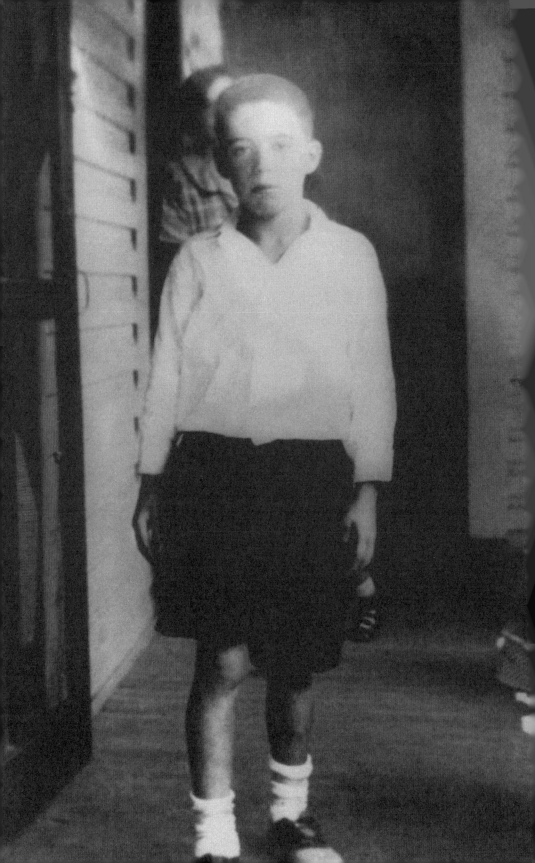

3 FINDING A PLACE IN THE WORLD

Chapter

❧

Henry grew up listening to adults talk about history, politics, and philosophy. Leonides Gonzalez's work at *La Prensa* brought him into contact with many Mexican and American intellectuals, and he often invited them to his home. They had deep, thoughtful conversations around the dinner table, and Henry was there to listen.

Leonides and Genoveva impressed upon their children the value of education. Henry knew education remained his key to a better life. After he graduated from Jefferson High School, he studied pre-engineering at San Antonio Junior College. In 1937, he earned his two-year degree.

Henry's brother Joaquin was going to school at the University of Texas in Austin, and Henry decided

Gonzalez grew up in this house on San Antonio's Upson Street.

to join him. He continued to study engineering, but times proved tough. The country was in the midst of the Great Depression, and jobs were scarce.

Henry worked odd jobs to pay for school, food, and a place to live with his brother. He cleaned rooms, served as a translator, and even worked for an exterminating company, where he earned $5 a week killing insects and other pests. However, the brothers' income covered only about one meal a day. They often went to bed cold and hungry.

When Henry fell ill, he decided to return home to San Antonio. He got well and enrolled in classes at St. Mary's University. His sister, Luz, often visited a college friend named Oralia Cuellar in Floresville, just southeast of San Antonio, and Henry usually drove her there. While Luz and Oralia visited, he had discovered that he had a lot in common with Oralia's sister Bertha. They both liked books and could talk for hours about the stories they had read.

When Bertha moved with her family to San Antonio, Henry got to know her even better. Both the Gonzalezes and Cuellars felt the young couple grew too serious about each other too quickly. They believed Henry and Bertha were too young to be in love, and the parents made plans that forced the couple to spend less time together.

However, neither Henry nor Bertha would let anyone break up their relationship. When Bertha fell ill with a lung disease called tuberculosis, Henry visited her every day. It was clear to see how devoted the young couple was to each other. After Bertha graduated from high school, the Gonzalezes and Cuellars agreed to let them get married. They started their life together November 23, 1940.

While Gonzalez worked toward completing a law degree at St. Mary's, he took odd jobs to help support himself and his new wife. The couple's first son, Henry Jr., was born in 1941, but he arrived prematurely. He only weighed 3 pounds (1.4 kilograms), and his parents worried for his well-being. However, with the help of his grandmother Genoveva, Henry Jr. would grow up healthy and strong.

Gonzalez lived his entire life in San Antonio, but politics took him to Austin, Texas, and Washington, D.C.

Later that same year, on December 7, the United States suffered a shocking attack. The Japanese bombed U.S. forces at Pearl Harbor in Hawaii, bringing the United States into World War II. Gonzalez was asked to work in military intelligence. He used his knowledge of the English, Spanish, and German languages to detect threats to the United States by working as a civilian cable and radio translator, interpreter, and censor for the U.S. military.

In August 1942, Bertha gave birth to Rose Mary. Eventually, the Gonzalezes would have eight children in their busy household. Gonzalez completed law school at St. Mary's the year after Rose Mary's birth.

In 1944, he went to work as an assistant juvenile probation officer for Bexar County, Texas, where he had lived most of his life. He worked with troubled kids, the boys and girls who committed serious felonies. The job sent him into his city's poor and struggling neighborhoods.

In his new position, Gonzalez strove to improve juvenile probation services in the Bexar County Juvenile Court system. He was tough when he had to be, but he also showed that he cared for troubled kids. He often brought boys to his house for a home-cooked meal before he dropped them off at the state reform school. In 1945, Gonzalez was promoted to chief probation officer. No other San Antonio agency was headed by a Mexican-American.

Despite his success, Gonzalez had to confront racism. As chief probation officer, he hired an African-American woman as a caseworker. But a local judge named Charles Anderson did not like this. He told Gonzalez the woman could not work in the courthouse, where the central

Throughout the 1940s, disease remained a huge problem for the Mexican-American community in San Antonio. In 1945, one of every 20 Hispanics suffered from tuberculosis. In 1946, two-thirds of all infant deaths in San Antonio were in the Hispanic community.

probation offices were located. Instead, the judge said, the woman would have to work on the east side of San Antonio, where most of the black citizens lived. Outraged, Gonzalez resigned. The judge did not want to lose him and end the progress he was making in cutting juvenile crime. Anderson changed his mind about the caseworker and asked Gonzalez to stay.

But he soon had another run-in with the judge. When one of the judge's friends sought a job in the probation department, Anderson expected Gonzalez to hire the man with no questions asked. Gonzalez was not pleased with the judge's friend, who used the word "punks" to describe all the boys the department dealt with. Gonzalez resigned again, this time for good.

"If I do not have the right to hire and fire, I am not interested in the position," he told Anderson.

Gonzalez's life then moved in a different direction. From 1947 through 1951, he helped his father with a Spanish-English translation business Leonides had started. Gonzalez took on other jobs at the same time, including serving as the executive secretary for the Pan American Progressive Association (PAPA) in 1947. PAPA was an organization that attempted to help people in need. He led efforts to overturn city regulations that limited opportunities for minorities to own property and

Rundown housing in a section of San Antonio that was home to many Mexican-Americans

build homes. PAPA fought these regulations all the way to the Supreme Court. In 1948, the court ruled that restrictions based on race, color, or creed were unconstitutional. Gonzalez also worked with the San Antonio Housing Authority, finding housing for families who lost their homes when their rundown neighborhoods were demolished.

Throughout his life, Gonzalez fought against racial discrimination and worked to make life better for the poor. Eventually, he decided there was one way he could make a bigger difference: politics. This would allow him to bring about the changes he desired. ✑

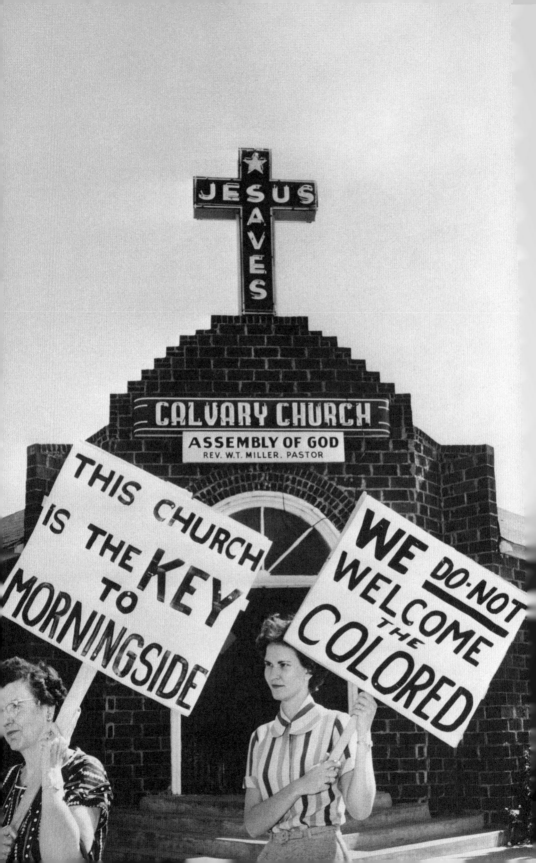

4 A POLITICAL CALLING

❧

Henry B. Gonzalez was up against more than a tough opponent when he first ran for city office. He was up against history: No Mexican-American had ever been elected to the job he was seeking. And he was up against the law: Texas' system made it difficult for Hispanics and African-Americans to vote. Still, Gonzalez dared to try.

As a probation officer and businessman, Gonzalez had gotten to know San Antonio well. He understood the problems in the community. He knew people at all levels of income. But he did not go into politics without a nudge.

In 1950, Gonzalez urged Gus Garcia, a successful Hispanic attorney, to run for office. Garcia was not interested. When Gonzalez kept after him, Garcia

Efforts to end racial segregation stirred tension in Texas and other Southern states during the 1950s.

snapped back, "You run yourself—leave me alone."

Gonzalez did run. He lost his first bid for a seat on the San Antonio City Council in 1950. But he had come close. His defeat by 2,000 votes was a much better result than many people expected. To some people, Gonzalez's effort was a sign of hope. It proved a Mexican-American could have a voice in politics.

He could have felt discouraged, but he didn't. Gonzalez kept on working to help others. He took a job with the city Housing Authority. In that role, he helped more than 400 families find new housing after they were forced out of their homes in San Antonio's slums.

During this time, Gonzalez's own family continued to grow. In 1951, Bertha gave birth to the couple's fifth child, a boy they named Stephen.

Gonzalez ran for the City Council again in 1953, and this time he won. He became the first Mexican-American ever elected to the San Antonio City Council.

Gonzalez put his heart and soul into his work, although the pay was meager. He made City Council issues his full-time job, but he earned no more than $1,040 a year as a councilman. That was hardly enough to support his large family, so he kept his translation business going. Still, he had to count on financial help from his family.

"There were no luxuries," Gonzalez's son Henry Jr. said about the early family years.

Gonzalez did not waste time trying to fit in on the council. He went right to work on issues important to his community, and he put desegregation at the top of that list. He had not forgotten the ban that kept him away from the city pool as a child. It was

Police lead two African-American students out of a Marshall, Texas, drug store after the two sought service at a whites-only lunch counter.

37

still in place, keeping nonwhites from the simple pleasure of cooling off on a hot summer day. He pushed to open the pools and other city facilities to people of all races.

Many people cheered him on as he worked to make sure all citizens of San Antonio had the same freedoms. Mexican-Americans and African-Americans supported his cause, as did a growing number of whites.

But not everyone liked what Gonzalez stood for, and they made sure he knew it. Some even threatened his life. He received death threats, and sometimes he faced more than tough talk. He recalled:

> *I came home late one night, when all of a sudden I heard something rev up and a car spun by in the darkness of the alley. And I heard two shots, and they hit the door of [my] car. I still believe if they wanted to, they could have hit me.*

On another occasion, Bertha heard her husband step onto the porch when a shot rang out. Fearing the worst, Bertha waited anxiously for Gonzalez to come in through the door. She waited and waited. When he didn't come, Bertha finally ventured out to look for him. She found him hiding in the dark. He was hoping the shooter would come back so he could get his license plate number.

Gonzalez refused to back down and continued to do his work. He became known as a leading—and sometimes loud—voice for liberal causes. He fought for fair housing practices and battled against discrimination in the law.

His critics said Gonzalez was a man who liked to see his name in headlines. They pointed to the time he went to the newspapers claiming someone tried to bribe him to keep quiet about crime problems in the city.

But Gonzalez answered his critics by quoting the French philosopher Charles Peguy: "He who failed to bellow the truth when he knew the truth is an accomplice of liars and cheats."

Restrictions that banned blacks, Latinos, and other nonwhites from many public places and limited their freedom were known as Jim Crow laws. The name came from a black character in a popular song from the 1830s. The song was a common part of what were known as minstrel shows. These shows featured white performers who smeared their faces with black soot and performed songs and dances that ridiculed black people. Such routines delighted white audiences of the time.

To Gonzalez, that meant keeping quiet about the truth was as bad as telling a lie.

Some political opponents tried to ruin him. They searched for anything that would make him look bad or damage his popularity. Once, the *San Antonio Light* newspaper ran a story about a woman who claimed Gonzalez had lied to her and taken her money. The woman said Gonzalez promised to defend her son in court. Gonzalez held no license to practice law, and such a promise would have been illegal.

The story outraged Gonzalez, who said it was a complete lie. Finally, another newspaper got the woman to admit she had never even met him. He later said:

Gonzalez won election to the Texas Senate for the first time in 1956.

I'm the only damn politician, and Mexican especially, who never took money to campaign for anybody—never will and never have. If you come up with something it's a frame-up. What I cannot stand is a frame-up. I'm alone in politics. I don't have any money. All I have is my name and my family.

In 1956, Gonzalez ran for a seat in the Texas Senate. Again, the battle would prove difficult. No Latino had served in that body since Texas' earliest days of statehood, more than a century earlier. When the votes rolled in, the results were very close. After the ballots were counted three times, the results showed Gonzalez won by 309 votes.

Despite his victory, Gonzalez was not welcomed with open arms at the Texas Legislature. But he did not let that bother him. He had dealt with prejudice before, and he was not about to let it stop him now. ℘

5 A New Voice

❦

Gonzalez did not quite fit in at the Texas Capitol. He was not one of the "good old boys," that much was sure. He was not interested in playing by the unspoken rules, which rewarded lawmakers who had been around the longest and encouraged newcomers to keep quiet and wait their turn. Some of his colleagues in the state Senate dismissed Gonzalez as "that Mexican," but Gonzalez was hard to ignore.

In 1954, the U.S. Supreme Court decided a landmark case called Brown v. Board of Education. The case centered on segregation in the schools of Topeka, Kansas, but the court's ruling affected the entire nation. The court decided racial segregation in public schools could not be allowed under the U.S. Constitution. The ruling meant public schools

Gonzalez's political career blossomed during his days at the Texas Capitol in Austin.

would have to be open to children of all colors. In many communities, especially throughout the South, that was not the case.

A 1954 ruling by the U.S. Supreme Court ended the practice of sending black and white students to separate public schools.

Those who didn't agree with the Supreme Court's decision took action. They wanted to get around the ruling and keep schools segregated. Texas schools had long been segregated, and many white lawmakers intended to keep them that way. In May 1957, the Texas Senate appeared ready to

pass 10 bills meant to skirt the court's ruling. The bills already had passed the state House of Representatives.

Gonzalez did not sit idly by when the bills reached the Senate. With the help of Senator Chick Kazen, Gonzalez railed against the proposed laws in the longest filibuster in Texas history.

"In those days, you had unlimited debate, and when you had the floor you could go on until (they) adjourn or you drop dead," Gonzalez said.

Kazen spoke for more than 12 hours before giving way to Gonzalez, who argued that it was time to leave behind racist policies and practices. Gonzalez talked and kept on talking, hoping his opponents would finally crack and drop the bills aimed at keeping Texas schools segregated.

"Once I had the floor, I was determined to hold onto it," he said. "They were determined to wait me out."

Gonzalez spoke about many things during those long hours, but he focused on some important ideas. He said that passing the bills would only lead back to the courts. He talked about what it was like to be

> *Throughout his life, Gonzalez loved to read. He quoted Greek and Roman writers when trying to make a point. He valued the opinions of others and regularly read newspapers from other countries to see what people elsewhere thought about key issues.*

a racial minority in the United States. He read from books describing racism's effects on blacks, Jews, and others. He reminded everyone of the important deeds of blacks and Hispanic Americans. He asked, "Did you know Negroes helped settle Texas? That a Negro died at the Alamo?"

Spectators filled the seats where the public could observe the Senate floor. Sometimes they broke into applause. Throughout the filibuster, the other senators came and went. Many couldn't believe Gonzalez was still talking when they returned. Some longtime politicians found Gonzalez's antics to be embarrassing. Those who wanted the racist bills passed grew angry. Yet Gonzalez didn't bow to scowling looks. He fought on with only his voice as a weapon.

"Finally about 4:30 in the morning they came over and said, 'Look, if you will let us pass just one, we will withdraw everything else,'" Gonzalez remembered. He agreed. Later, he helped see that this single bill was never passed into law either.

While serving as a legislator in Austin, Gonzalez commuted more than 80 miles (128 kilometers) each way every day while the Senate was in session. When he was home, he was often too tired to spend much time with his family. This was especially true when Gonzalez was faced with a major struggle in the Senate.

Gonzalez in front of the Texas Capitol in Austin in 1957

"People don't understand that when you fili-buster you have a bad, bad case of just a raw throat," Gonzalez's son Charles said. "Dad would come home in a total state of exhaustion. If we had something we wanted to talk to him about, it just wasn't going to happen. He couldn't talk, he was so tired. I remember him just crawling upstairs to go to bed and having to rest before he could eat."

Though his schedule at the Texas Capitol was busy, Gonzalez showed devotion to his family. He taught his children how to swim, and he enjoyed spending whatever time he had with them. "Dad sacrificed quantity time by being in politics, but we had quality time that made up the difference," Henry Jr. said.

Charles, who followed his father's footsteps into politics, said:

Gonzalez with his wife, Bertha, (in white hat), his sister, Luz Tamez, and three of his children in the Texas Senate chamber

That is the greatest memory I have. It's not this big spectacular family vacation and it's not about Disneyland. The neat experiences are the down times, the throwing of the football, watching you, helping you with a lesson.

The family stuck together, too. When they found the chance, they packed up their car and went camping on Padre Island, located along the Gulf Coast in southern Texas. Bertha and the children also helped with Gonzalez's political career. They stuffed letters into envelopes for political mailings and did whatever they could do to help.

In 1958, Gonzalez's young political career took a surprising turn. After just two years as a state lawmaker, he decided to run for governor of Texas. With little chance to win, Gonzalez knew at least his campaign would break down a barrier. He was the first Mexican-American to run for governor.

Gonzalez had come into conflict with Governor Price Daniel more than once since joining the state Senate. They had butted heads regarding the governor's selection to fill a judgeship in Gonzalez's part

> *Located on the southern Texas coast, Padre Island ranks as a popular recreational area and wildlife habitat. The island got its name from the Spanish priest Padre Nicolas Balli, who operated a ranch there in the early 1800s with his nephew.*

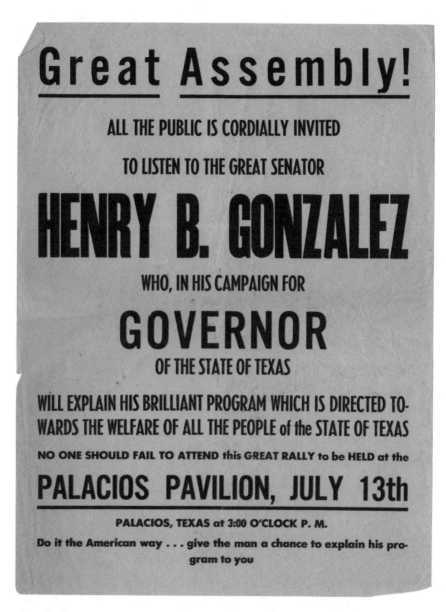

Great Assembly!

ALL THE PUBLIC IS CORDIALLY INVITED

TO LISTEN TO THE GREAT SENATOR

HENRY B. GONZALEZ

WHO, IN HIS CAMPAIGN FOR

GOVERNOR

OF THE STATE OF TEXAS

WILL EXPLAIN HIS BRILLIANT PROGRAM WHICH IS DIRECTED TOWARDS THE WELFARE OF ALL THE PEOPLE of the STATE OF TEXAS

NO ONE SHOULD FAIL TO ATTEND this GREAT RALLY to be HELD at the

PALACIOS PAVILION, JULY 13th

PALACIOS, TEXAS at 3:00 O'CLOCK P. M.

Do it the American way . . . give the man a chance to explain his program to you

Gonzalez lost his campaign to be governor of Texas.

of the state. And they had tangled about issues related to ending segregation in Texas' public schools. But Gonzalez did not run for governor because he expected to win. He ran because he did not want Daniel to glide into a second term without being challenged or without having to defend his positions on key issues.

Behind the wheel of his station wagon, Gonzalez traveled the state and met as many people as possible, despite more attempts to intimidate him and more threats on his life.

In only two weeks, Gonzalez put 14,000 miles (22,400 km) on the family car. He gave speeches anywhere he could. He criticized Daniel's record as governor, and he explained what he wanted for Texas. He wanted to wipe out all traces of segregation in the state. He wanted to send more poor students to college. And he wanted taxes on natural gas pipelines but not on sales or income.

Though he lost the election, Gonzalez won national attention, including that of a young senator from Massachusetts named John F. Kennedy. Gonzalez and Kennedy had met before. They crossed paths in the early 1950s, when Gonzalez served as deputy director of the San Antonio Housing Authority and Kennedy was a member of the U.S. House of Representatives. Gonzalez later recalled Kennedy:

> *He was a mostly unknown Congressman.*
> *I saw and identified with something*

beneath his shyness: a decency, a concern, a strength. ... He in Washington, and I down in San Antonio, were on a parallel path—each working in our own way, in far distant places, toward the same general goals—though his were better defined than mine, and his vision far greater.

When Kennedy decided to run for president of the United States, Gonzalez wanted to help. Along with Dennis Chavez, a U.S. senator from New Mexico, Gonzalez served as national co-chair of the Viva Kennedy campaigns in 1960, urging Mexican-Americans to vote for the Massachusetts Democrat. Gonzalez said:

People will respond to you if they can believe what you say. People will trust you if you keep your word. People will respect you if you respect yourself. If you lay out the problem accurately and if you propose a reasonable solution, people will give you a chance, not withstanding your heritage or race. Some would never vote for the Irish Kennedy or the Mexican Gonzalez; and some would only vote for us because he was Irish and I am Mexican; but most would decide the issues on the merits, and us on our ability.

Gonzalez was right. In November, Kennedy was elected president. At the same time, Gonzalez won a second term in the Texas Senate. But he would not be in Austin for long. He was about to follow Kennedy to Washington, D.C. ☙

John F. Kennedy sought the support of Hispanic voters during his 1960 campaign.

Chapter

6 Henry B. Goes to Washington

The road Henry Gonzalez took to Washington, D.C., began with a bumpy stretch. He had to endure defeat before making his way to the nation's capital.

Texas Senator Lyndon B. Johnson had been John F. Kennedy's running mate in the 1960 presidential election. After Kennedy won, Johnson left his seat in the U.S. Senate and became vice president. A special election was required to replace him. Gonzalez decided to run, but his campaign was not successful.

A Republican won the seat, which was a disappointment to the new Democratic president and vice president. Gonzalez managed to win only a small fraction of the vote statewide in a race that included several candidates. But in his corner of Texas, around San Antonio, Gonzalez collected the most

Gonzalez stands in front of the U.S. Capitol in Washington, D.C.

votes of anyone. Clearly, the voters who knew him best liked and supported him, even if the rest of Texas rejected him.

Gonzalez still had a job to do at the state Capitol as a member of the Texas Senate. But soon he saw another chance to get to Congress. In 1961, the representative from Gonzalez's part of Texas was selected by Kennedy to become a judge. The congressman resigned, and a special election was scheduled to fill that position. Gonzalez was ready to run for office again.

Kennedy backed Gonzalez, and the president's younger brother Robert went to Texas to help the campaign. Vice President Johnson also returned to Texas and gave speeches supporting Gonzalez in the closing days of the campaign. On November 4, 1961, voters went to the polls in record numbers. More than 95,000 votes were cast, and Gonzalez won a clear victory.

Gonzalez would represent the 20th District of Texas in the U.S. House of Representatives, but his victory was important to people far beyond his district. He was the first Mexican-American that Texas had ever sent to Congress, and his state was a

> *In the November 4, 1961, election, Gonzalez garnered more than 52,800 votes. His opponent, John Goode Jr., received more than 42,500 votes. At the time, the total number of votes was the highest ever cast in a special election in San Antonio.*

center of the nation's Hispanic population. He was used to blazing new trails. He had done so on the San Antonio City Council and in the Texas Senate. But this election was even more significant.

In the 1960s, the United States experienced tense battles regarding civil rights, which are the most basic rights to participate in a democracy. They give people the chance to vote, to speak their minds, and to do simple things like eat at the restaurant of their choice. In debates on civil rights, Gonzalez would be a voice in Congress for Hispanics. He also hoped to be a voice for all minorities and for poor people across the country.

President John F. Kennedy (second from left) with Hispanic Congressmen Joseph Montoya (left), Edward Roybal, and Henry B. Gonzalez.

When Gonzalez was sworn in to the U.S. House of Representatives, he raised his right hand and took the oath just as his peers had done. But he held something important in his left hand. It was a piece of paper, a bill that called for the end of poll taxes.

In some parts of the country, voters were charged a tax or fee at the polls. This meant they were paying for the right to vote. Poll taxes discouraged poor people from voting. The taxes had been used in Texas and other states to keep Mexican-Americans, African-Americans, and other minority groups away from the polls. Gonzalez's first act in

Laws that segregated schools and limited the rights of racial minorities affected people in many states.

Segregation in 1950
- Segregation required
- Segregation permitted
- Segregation prohibited
- No segregation legislation

0   400 miles
0   400 kilometers

Congress was to offer his bill to ban poll taxes.

That bill would eventually become part of the Voting Rights Act, aimed at protecting the right of all people to take part in free elections. But the four years until then would be full of challenges and struggles. When Gonzalez first came to Washington, D.C., new congressmen were expected to learn the system quietly. Just as it was at the Texas Capitol, more experienced lawmakers expected new ones to wait their turn. But that had not been Gonzalez's style in Austin, and it would not be his style in Washington.

Gonzalez had gone to the nation's capital to serve his country and his constituents, and that was what he set out to do—regardless of whom it offended. As he had in Austin, he dressed in brightly colored suits that stood out in the halls of Congress. And he continued to speak in a loud and confident voice.

In 1963, Gonzalez got involved in a dispute that demonstrated the tense feelings in the country at the time. A Texas Republican and fellow congressman named Ed Foreman was upset by votes cast by Gonzalez and several other members of the House. Foreman called them all "pinkos," which was a slur meaning communist or someone who sympathized with communists.

There were few insults more damaging in the

United States at the time. The nation was locked in a political struggle with the Soviet Union, the world's most powerful communist country. The dispute had nearly turned into an all-out war when the Soviets tried to send atomic warheads to Cuba. To call somebody a "pinko" was the same as saying he was un-American or unpatriotic.

Gonzalez did not sit still in the face of such criticism. In fact, his temper flared. He urged Foreman to settle matters outside of the House chambers. When the two were face to face, Gonzalez, who had boxed as a young man, took a swipe at Foreman. The blow missed its mark and landed on Foreman's shoulder, but Gonzalez had made his point. Foreman backed off in his criticism, and Gonzalez later helped a fellow Democrat defeat Foreman at the polls.

Gonzalez had shown that he was not going to be pushed around. But he was usually a patient and open person. He liked to spend time in the shops and restaurants of San Antonio talking with the people he represented. And while he worked hard to end racist policies, he never supported violent ways of opposing discrimination.

The tension and violence in the United States in the 1960s reached its worst point on November 22, 1963. President Kennedy and his wife, Jacqueline, visited Texas, and Gonzalez was among the lawmakers who traveled with them throughout the state. He

introduced the president during an event in San Antonio, and he applauded with the crowd when the first lady greeted the people in Spanish. Gonzalez was along when the Kennedys next went to Dallas, and he was riding several cars behind the president when shots rang out. Gonzalez's vehicle was part of the motorcade that raced to the hospital, where he found out the president had been killed.

Gonzalez traveled with the Kennedys during their tragic trip to Texas in November 1963.

As the 1960s wore on, Gonzalez stood up against violence even when his opinion was unpopular. During those years, some of the leaders of protest groups decided they needed to be militant, or to use violence to pursue their goals. The Mexican American Youth Organization, known as MAYO, was one group that accepted a radical strategy. The group's leaders publicly criticized Gonzalez for being too soft and too easy on whites. The young activists said violence might be necessary to overcome gringos, or whites.

Gonzalez during his early days in Congress

Gonzalez believed groups such as MAYO were wrong to spread messages of hate against whites. Seeking equality for Mexican-Americans by spreading such hate was a mistake, he said. "Mr. Speaker, there is no greater poison of mind and spirit than race hate," Gonzalez said in a speech on the floor of the House of Representatives. "There is no greater evil among men than the irrational antipathy that is based in race and race alone."

The speech became one of the best known in Gonzalez's 37 years in Congress. He talked about the terrible injustice of being considered a lesser person merely because of race. He expressed his alarm at groups such as MAYO, saying they may have had worthy goals, but they had "fallen into the spell and trap of reverse racism." As a result, Gonzalez said, they had become what they claimed to hate: violent racists. He declared, "[T]hey are themselves the ultimate tragedy of racism."

He also said that he believed in the U.S. system of government and that the majority of Americans wanted fairness for all people. He believed his voters in San Antonio proved that by electing him to office again and again. He told fellow congressmen:

> All my political life I have asked that I be judged for my qualifications, for my policies, for my proposals, not on what I am, or what my name may be. I ask for every man that he be given that same privilege.

Though racism still exists today, Gonzalez used nonviolent methods—taking action in his role in Congress—to seek an end to discrimination. In 1964, he threw his support behind the landmark Civil Rights Act, which promised all races equality in American society. He was one of few Southern congressmen to do so, but the bill still passed.

Throughout his time in Washington, Gonzalez lived modestly. While some congressmen kept fancy residences or went out to expensive dinners, he lived in a small apartment, which he filled with

Gonzalez often passed out handbills decorated with an eagle and a quote from Henry Cabot Lodge (1850-1924), the late senator from Massachusetts. The quote read, in part, "[L]et us have done with British-Americans and Irish-Americans and German-Americans, and so on, and all be Americans. If a man is going to be an American at all let him be so without adjectives; and if he is going to be something else, let him drop the word American from his personal description."

books, and he traveled home nearly every weekend. He would see his family and visit with constituents, talking with his neighbors, barbers, and gas station attendants. He urged other members of Congress to do the same:

> Get out of Washington. Find out what the people are doing. See how they are living. Visit lines in unemployment offices. Visit the places where free food is passed out. Sit for a day in a juvenile court. Visit jails. Go to a national park and see how foresight and planning have saved our natural resources. It could do the same for human resources. Walk around slums and talk with the people who live in them. It is a sad fact, but many people who go to Europe won't drive three miles to see what it's like on the other side of town.

The "everyday" people of Gonzalez's district helped him make decisions on issues he faced in Washington. He never forgot who elected him to office, as his friend Bill Sinkin later recalled:

I was at Henry B.'s house one Christmas Day, along with a few other friends and supporters when the doorbell rang. Henry opened it, and there was a man standing there. This man took a bus across town, probably spent his last ten cents, to give Henry a Christmas present—a 10-cent Christmas card. Henry invited the man in, sat him down, gave him breakfast and kept everyone waiting for forty-five minutes. Just took him in like he was his biggest contributor. That showed where his priorities were.

Gonzalez's long career in Congress had just begun in the 1960s, but the turmoil of that decade

Gonzalez with Anna, the youngest of his eight children

had a major impact on him. Later, Gonzalez said one of his biggest mistakes came not long after Kennedy's assassination.

Lyndon B. Johnson had moved into the presidency, and he wanted to expand U.S. involvement in a growing conflict in the Southeast Asian country of Vietnam. The president, Gonzalez later said, pressured him into voting for the Gulf of Tonkin resolution in 1964. The resolution opened the way for the country's headlong dive into the Vietnam War. The war lasted for years, costing thousands of American

President Lyndon B. Johnson (right) applauds as Gonzalez speaks during a 1965 rally.

lives and millions of Vietnamese lives. In the end, the United States was unable to keep Vietnam from communist rule.

The president did not really need Gonzalez's vote to pass the resolution. The matter sailed through the House. Still, the decision to support the president on Vietnam was one that Gonzalez regretted. It was also a learning experience early in his congressional career.

"I never had graver doubts, and I swore that no matter who it offended, or anything, I would never vote out of fear again," Gonzalez said.

Gonzalez went on to a long career in Congress that was marked by his devotion to a few core beliefs and his willingness to challenge people who abused their power. He fought for Americans who lacked good homes and good jobs, and he remained a voice for those who he believed needed one most. ℘

7 A Hero for the Homeless

Housing was a key issue throughout Gonzalez's long public career. His concern about housing began when he was a young man growing up on the west side of San Antonio, where many poor families lived in rundown homes. Gonzalez knew the issue well from his days with the San Antonio Housing Authority, and he believed the government had a role to play in making sure people had a chance to live in decent housing. As a congressman, he could help make this dream come true for many people.

Gonzalez worked with President Johnson on the Model Cities program in the 1960s. The program came along when inner cities were in bad shape. Many American cities were struggling with crime, poor housing, and high unemployment. The program

President Johnson (right) and Gonzalez greet each other at a bill-signing ceremony.

aimed to ease poverty, discrimination, and problems of inadequate housing.

Model Cities took on issues that played a role in creating these problems, such as the need for better public transportation, community health services, day care, assistance for the elderly, and programs to help people stay in the workforce. Some cities had all of these problems and more.

President Johnson shows off a freshly signed bill aimed at solving the problem of poverty in America.

The Model Cities program was part of Johnson's sweeping plan for America called the Great Society. In his plan, Johnson proposed many changes in law. He wanted to stamp out poverty across the country, from the tiny towns to the huge cities. Johnson's plans aimed at the factors that made people poor or kept them that way. For example, the president's Great Society plans provided health care for senior citizens and the poor. The plan also provided money to improve public schools. Gonzalez was a key supporter of Johnson's plans to build new and better public housing. In fact, Johnson invited Gonzalez to be at the ceremony where the president signed those Great Society measures into law.

Gonzalez's work on housing issues lasted throughout his decades in Washington, D.C. In 1981, he was named chairman of the House Subcommittee on Housing and Community Development. He battled then-President Ronald Reagan, who called for cuts in funding for public housing projects. Gonzalez would do the same against President George H.W. Bush, who followed Reagan into the White House.

While these presidents wanted

Lyndon B. Johnson, also a Texas Democrat, served as vice president under President John F. Kennedy. When Kennedy was assassinated, Johnson became president. In 1964, voters elected Johnson to a full term as president. He chose not to run for reelection in 1968.

to reduce the government's spending on housing, Gonzalez continued to look for new solutions to housing problems. In the 1980s, he led efforts to put more money into housing. He pushed through new laws that aimed to help homeless people and to provide housing for people with AIDS, which was then a new and misunderstood illness affecting thousands of Americans.

Gonzalez was recognized for his work. In 1991, he earned the National Alliance to End Homelessness Award for Public Sector Achievement. In 1996, he garnered the Housing Assistance Council Special Award. The following year, he was named the recipient of the Fair Housing Award. Gonzalez's work on housing issues was not limited to problems in cities. He was also concerned about problems in small-town America, and in 1992, he won the National Rural Housing Legislator of the Year award.

Gonzalez was something of a loner in Washington, D.C. He spent his evenings in his office, often working late into the night on housing and other issues close to his heart. He kept careful watch over all the letters his office received from people back in Texas and others around the country. He wanted to sign each letter sent from his office, instead of using an "auto pen," which many officials used. He lived in a tiny apartment near the Capitol so he wouldn't have far to walk after his late nights

SAN ANTONIO CHANI
IMPROVEMENT PROJ

UNIT IV

ALAZAN CREI

PART II

SPONSORED BY

ANTONIO RIVER AUT

RUCTION UNDER SUP

OF

Y ENGINEER D

ORT WORTH

AL CONTRACT

IN BR

at the office. He returned home to San Antonio on weekends, where he, his wife, and their eight children had lunch together every Sunday.

Sometimes after the food was gone, Gonzalez would set a stack of letters on the table. He would sign them one by one, and his children would slide the letters into envelopes and seal them. The family worked together until all the letters were ready to go. Then they could head into the yard for some free time together. ℘

Gonzalez led efforts to improve life in San Antonio, including work to protect clean water and prevent floods.

73

MR. GONZALEZ
SUBCOMMITTEE
CHAIRMAN

Chapter

8 A FEARLESS LEADER

❦

Early in his career, Gonzalez quickly became a strong voice in Congress, and he was a leader in the decades to follow. He continued to champion programs that helped the poor lead better lives. He took on issues that others wanted to avoid. He spoke his mind even when his ideas were unpopular. He shed light on problems he believed Americans needed to know about and deal with.

Early on, Gonzalez focused on a program that allowed Mexican workers into the United States and then let them suffer in terrible conditions. The bracero program began in the World War II era and lasted into the 1960s. Foreign workers, many of them Mexican, were allowed into the country at first because of a shortage of farmworkers. Once in the

Gonzalez took on leadership roles in the U.S. House of Representatives.

Mexican farm-workers sit awaiting work assignments.

United States, the Mexican workers lived in shacks without proper systems for sewage and other waste. They earned small wages. They lived without proper nutrition. Gonzalez worked to end the program and the abuses it allowed.

Later, Gonzalez took on more issues important to him personally and to all Americans. In 1977, he was chosen as chair of the House Assassinations Committee. The committee was created to investigate the murders of President John F. Kennedy and civil rights leader Martin Luther King Jr.

The task was close to Gonzalez's heart. He had been there when Kennedy was assassinated in 1963. And Gonzalez shared many of King's goals later in the 1960s. King was a well-known leader in the push for civil rights, and he urged African-Americans to use nonviolent protest to win fair treatment under U.S. law. Like Kennedy, King had been assassinated. He was gunned down in 1968 while he stood on a motel balcony in Memphis, Tennessee.

After Kennedy's death, Gonzalez had continued the fight for the causes he and Kennedy believed in, and he kept a photograph of the late president on his wall throughout his many years in Congress.

The identity of Kennedy's gunman—Lee Harvey Oswald—had been known almost immediately, but many questions about the killing remained. People wondered why the killer had done it and who else might have been involved in plotting the assassination. Similar questions surrounded King's case.

Gonzalez hoped that the House Assassinations Committee could get to the bottom of Kennedy's and King's deaths, but he ended up walking away in

In 1964, a government panel called the Warren Commission investigated the assassination of President John F. Kennedy. The commission concluded that Lee Harvey Oswald acted alone in shooting the president. In 1978, the House Assassinations Committee disagreed. The committee concluded that Kennedy was likely killed as a result of a conspiracy, meaning others had helped plan and carry out the shooting. Many people disagreed with the committee's findings.

Gonzalez stands with his father, Leonides, President Kennedy (left), and Vice President Johnson (right) in the summer of 1963. Gonzalez would later investigate the president's death.

disappointment. He resigned from the committee. He believed organized crime was blocking the investigation, and he decided the committee was not capable of finding the truth. "I've had it with that miserable clot of yo-yos," Gonzalez said.

In 1989, he was elected chairman of the House Banking, Finance and Urban Affairs Committee. He had already served for 27 years as a member of this important committee. As chairman, he focused on the needs of everyday citizens, rather than worrying about bankers and financial giants. Gonzalez worked hard to pass legislation dealing with many issues, including bank fraud, flood insurance reform, housing problems, and help for small businesses.

He also led efforts to clean up a mess he had seen coming years before others did. Throughout the 1980s, he had predicted trouble in the savings and loan industry. Savings and loan associations were something like banks, but they fell under different laws. In the late 1980s, one savings and loan after another failed. The failures were caused by mismanagement, increasing interest rates, and sometimes fraud. Many savings and loans had been run by people who put their customers at great risk to enrich themselves. Those customers, many of them everyday citizens, lost money—even their life savings, putting families at great risk.

Gonzalez led the government effort to repair the damage. He pushed for the passage of bills that bailed out failed savings and loan associations, repaying people who had lost their savings. The bailout cost the government more than $200 billion. Gonzalez also pushed new laws to prevent similar problems in the future.

The savings and loan crisis again demonstrated traits Gonzalez showed throughout his career. He was not afraid to be a lone voice fighting the crowd. And he was not afraid to take on powerful people, even ones in his own party.

In dealing with this crisis, Gonzalez heaped scorn on a savings and loan owner named Charles Keating of Phoenix, Arizona, and five U.S. senators, four of whom were Democrats like Gonzalez. He accused the senators of corruption because of their ties to Keating. The five had received donations from Keating and had then protected him from government regulators. An agency of the federal government had been looking into Keating's savings and loan before it collapsed, but the senators urged the government officials to back off. That gave Keating the freedom to continue his dubious way of doing business.

Keating headed American Continental Corporation, which acquired Lincoln Savings of California, and stood accused of fraud and other violations of the law. He was convicted of the charges in 1993, though his conviction was overturned about four years later. Eventually, Keating admitted to committing bankruptcy fraud by taking $1 million from his corporation. He knew his savings and loan was about to crumble, but still he took the money for himself.

Gonzalez angered some members of his party because he was attacking fellow Democrats with ties to Keating. Some lawmakers in his party even tried to remove Gonzalez from his chairmanship, but he stood strong. When the dust cleared, Gonzalez had cleaned up the savings and loan industry, and he had kept his post leading the banking committee.

Charles Keating led a failed savings and loan and lost millions of dollars for his customers.

U.S. Representative Joe Kennedy, nephew of the late president, served on the committee with Gonzalez and looked to him as a mentor:

> *Believe me, folks, in Washington, D.C., these days we don't have enough Henry B. Gonzalezes. We need to have people who are willing to stand up to the corruption, who are willing to stand up to the various powers that be in America.*

Gonzalez soon took on another Washington scandal, which became known as Iraqgate. The nation of Iraq had gone to war with neighboring Iran. Because the United States also considered Iran an enemy, the U.S. government saw Iraq as a sort of ally. Gonzalez discovered that the United States had helped Saddam Hussein, the dictator of Iraq, by issuing more than $3 billion in loans and letters of credit. The money was supposedly for agricultural products, but in reality Hussein used it to buy weapons.

Those weapons would eventually be used in Iraq's 1990 invasion of Kuwait. That meant weapons paid for with American money would be used against American troops in the first Gulf War, when U.S. soldiers fought the Iraqis and pushed them out of Kuwait.

Gonzalez was outraged when the 1991 war began. He said he wanted the American people to *Fellow Texans* know how their money had been used. He also *Henry Gonzalez* *and President* called for the impeachment of President George *George H.W.* *Bush* H.W. Bush for his part in Iraqgate, but his plea was

ignored by the majority of those in Congress. Years earlier, Gonzalez had called for the impeachment of President Reagan after he sent U.S. troops into the island nation of Grenada. That call also found little support in Congress.

Very late in his career, Gonzalez came to the defense of another president who was at risk of being forced from office. President Bill Clinton faced impeachment and stood accused of lying while under oath. Clinton had not been forthcoming about a relationship he had with a White House intern.

Gonzalez said this incident revolved around a private matter, whereas his previous calls for the impeachment of Reagan and Bush involved issues related to the U.S. Constitution—mainly that those presidents had sent troops into battle without the approval of Congress. "This is a personal flaw and a failure on the part of the president. It's of a moral nature, not political," Gonzalez said of the Clinton scandal.

His vote against Clinton's impeachment would be his last. ✑

> *The United States and several Caribbean nations sent troops into Grenada in 1983. The invasion took place after communist rebels had taken over Grenada's government and killed the prime minister. President Ronald Reagan said the U.S. invasion was necessary to protect Americans living in the country. The rebels were forced out of power. The year after the invasion, Grenada held elections to choose a new government.*

Chapter 9

HONORED FOR COURAGE

⤷❦⤶

During his political career, Henry Gonzalez faced everything from harsh criticism to threats on his life. He continued to battle hard for what he believed in, regardless of the cost to himself.

He also proved he would not put party loyalty ahead of fairness and honesty. While he called for the impeachment of two Republican presidents, he also brought attention to what he believed were the misdeeds of senators—the "Keating Five"—four of whom were Democrats.

For his fearlessness and honesty, Gonzalez earned the 1994 Profile in Courage Award from the John F. Kennedy Library. Before he was president, Kennedy wrote a book called *Profiles in Courage*, which told the stories of eight senators who had

Gonzalez's long career in Congress made him one of Washington's most familiar faces.

John Kennedy Jr. and sister, Caroline (left), present an award to Gonzalez, whose wife stands at his side.

shown true courage in their conduct. They were the sort of leaders who put what was right ahead of what was popular. The Profile in Courage Award has been given since 1989 to people who demonstrate a similar commitment.

When receiving the honor, Gonzalez was cited for his courage in dealing with the savings and loan industry and the Iraq scandal. The award was especially meaningful to Gonzalez, who had helped get President Kennedy elected, had been there when his friend was shot, and had served on the committee investigating that assassination.

Despite America's imperfections and his work to

address them, Gonzalez never failed to point out that people in many other countries didn't live as well as Americans. He had files in his office filled with the names of people from Latin America who wanted to move to his country. "Their relatives in San Antonio are asking me to please help them get into the United States," he said.

Gonzalez also stressed that democracy takes work. He believed that the future of the United States depended on people's willingness to be tolerant of one another and to focus on their common goals instead of their differences, whether they were racial, religious, or political. "If we want to tear our society apart, we can do it easily," he said. "Nobody has mandated that the United States will be preserved. We've got to make it work."

Through the years, Gonzalez earned the respect even of those who opposed his views. During his 37 years in Congress, he rarely faced a serious threat in any campaign for reelection. No Democrat ever stepped forward to challenge him for the party's

Other people who have earned the Profile in Courage Award include Sima Samar, Afghanistan's first women's affairs minister; Dan Ponder Jr., a state representative from Georgia who defended his state's law targeting racial hate crimes; and former President Gerald Ford, who helped heal the country in the days following the Watergate scandal, which forced President Richard Nixon to resign from office.

endorsement. He faced a Republican opponent in only six elections. His constituents stood firmly behind him, often granting him at least 80 percent of their votes. Columnist Jim Eskin said this of Gonzalez:

> *He never lost sight of the fact that he worked for the people. Henry B. walked with political legends like JFK and LBJ. But he knew his real job was to walk with average citizens. Throughout a remarkable career, he consistently demonstrated political courage, honesty and integrity.*

Gonzalez in a family portrait with his wife, Bertha, and their eight children in about 1960

Gonzalez also made sure no one could ever

Gonzalez's campaign signs were a common sight in his district, where he was reelected 18 times.

accuse him of being influenced by money. Unlike many others in politics, Gonzalez wouldn't accept any contributions from political groups that might have wanted to sway his opinion. He remained proud of his clean reputation:

> *I walked through the mud of San Antonio politics. I walked through the mud of state politics in Austin. And for thirty years I've walked through the mud in Washington, D.C., and I still haven't gotten the tips of my shoes dirty.*

Chapter

10 A LASTING IMPACT

&∽⌢∽&

In the late 1990s, some Democrats began talking about replacing Gonzalez. He had been in Congress for more than three decades and was moving into his 80s. He had lost his committee chairmanship when Republicans swept the 1994 elections and won a majority of seats in the House of Representatives. Younger members of Gonzalez's own party wondered if he was too old to do his job anymore. The feisty Texan told his colleagues what he thought about their opinions:

> *I have served with honor and integrity and success. I have never failed myself, and I have never failed you.*

Gonzalez continued to serve his district, but he couldn't go on forever. He was still the senior

A portrait of Gonzalez now hangs in the U.S. Capitol.

Democrat on the banking committee he had once chaired when he began to have health problems. In 1997, he announced his plans to retire. That year, he had to be rushed from the floor of the House of Representatives and taken to a hospital. An infection had caused damage to his heart, and his health remained fragile for months to come. "After being in political contests for almost half a century, I have run my last political race," Gonzalez said.

Friends and opponents reacted to his upcoming retirement with words of praise. "Few members of Congress have had a more distinguished congressional career in this century than Henry Gonzalez," said Jim Leach, a Republican representative from Iowa who hadn't always seen eye to eye with Gonzalez. "I know of none more honorable."

Gonzalez during his final year in office

Gonzalez returned to San Antonio to recover and rebuild his strength after his heart problems. He was away from the Capitol for more than a year. In September 1998, he came back to Washington, D.C., to finish out his term, which would be the last of his 19 terms in Congress. During his final days in office, Gonzalez got the chance to look back on his career and his occasional role as the lone voice willing to speak up against injustice, abuses of power, and even the will of his own party. He addressed fellow lawmakers:

> *I was something of a curiosity, being the only so-called ethnic minority member of my delegation. I was accepted as a peer, but that was not to say I felt welcomed. And I stand before you today, accepted, but seen by some as an inconvenience and unwelcome obstacle.*

Gonzalez went back home to San Antonio to his wife, eight children, and grandchildren. His remaining time with them, however, would be short. When Gonzalez woke early November 28, 2000, he was running a fever and felt thirsty. He went to Baptist Medical Center, where he died that afternoon, surrounded by his family. He was 84.

His funeral was held at San Fernando Cathedral, the church where he'd been baptized as a child. The funeral Mass was celebrated in English and Spanish. More than 1,100 people came to pay their respects. Because the church could only hold 600 people, the Mass was televised next door at City Hall.

At the church, mourners received small cards as

mementos. The cards featured a photograph of Gonzalez above some of his famous quotes. One spoke to labels put on people, such as Mexican-American, African-American, or Irish-American: "I am an American without prefix, suffix, apology or any other kind of modification."

Another quote reminded everyone of his hope and commitment to unify Americans of all races and religions: "I never believed that the way to win equality is through separation."

Americans all across the country mourned Gonzalez's death. Flowers, cards, and letters poured in from friends, constituents, and others whose lives he had touched. Regrets also came from politicians—both Republicans and Democrats alike—including George W. Bush, who was then the governor of Texas, and President Bill Clinton. "I am especially grateful for his friendship and his steadfast support for me as a person," Clinton wrote.

As Gonzalez's body was taken from the church for burial, a mariachi band played a sad song in the cathedral. Mourners, some crying and some applauding, lined the streets between the church and the cemetery where Gonzalez would be buried. Some held signs thanking Gonzalez for all he had done.

"To those who supported him, Gonzalez was a man of integrity, honor, courage, and strength, who cared for the people he represented," said Andy

Hernandez of St. Mary's University in San Antonio. "He was one of the very first extraordinary leaders of the Mexican-American generation who battled segregation. He himself broke through barriers."

When Gonzalez retired from politics in 1998, his son Charles stepped in and won election to the U.S. House seat held so long by his father. His political career was just getting started when his father died.

"Dad was on a mission," Charles said. "He never forgot a person nor an issue. He had an incredible memory. He opened eyes, he opened hearts, and that shall be my father's legacy." ❧

Representative Charles Gonzalez took over his father's seat in the U.S. Congress.

95

GONZALEZ'S LIFE

1916
Henry Gonzalez
is born May 3 in
San Antonio,
Texas

1937
Graduates from
San Antonio
Junior College

1940
Marries
Bertha Cuellar

1941
Serves as an inter-
preter and censor for
the U.S. military
during World War II

1915

1940

1916
German-born physi-
cist Albert Einstein
publishes his general
theory of relativity

1939
German troops invade
Poland; Britain and
France declare war
on Germany; World
War II (1939-1945)
begins

WORLD EVENTS

1943
Completes law degree
at St. Mary's
University

1945
Works as the chief
probation officer of
Bexar County, Texas

1950
Loses election for
seat on the San
Antonio City Council

1945

1945
The United
Nations is
founded

1949
Birth of the
People's Republic
of China

GONZALEZ'S LIFE

1953
Wins election to the San Antonio City Council

1956
Elected to the Texas Senate

1958
Loses campaign as the first Mexican-American to run for Texas governor

Great Assembly!
ALL THE PUBLIC IS CORDIALLY INVITED
TO LISTEN TO THE GREAT SENATOR
HENRY B. GONZALEZ
WHO, IN HIS CAMPAIGN FOR
GOVERNOR
OF THE STATE OF TEXAS
WILL EXPLAIN HIS BRILLIANT PROGRAM WHICH IS DIRECTED TOWARDS THE WELFARE OF ALL THE PEOPLE of the STATE OF TEXAS
NO ONE SHOULD FAIL TO ATTEND this GREAT RALLY to be HELD at the
PALACIOS PAVILION, JULY 13th
PALACIOS, TEXAS at 3:45 O'CLOCK P. M.
Do it the American way . . . give the man a chance to explain his program to you

1955

1953
The first Europeans climb Mount Everest

1959
Fidel Castro becomes president of Cuba

WORLD EVENTS

1960

Co-chairs the Viva Kennedy campaign urging Mexican-Americans to vote for John F. Kennedy

1961

Elected to fill vacancy in U.S. House of Representatives

1963

Rides in presidential motorcade when Kennedy is assassinated in Dallas, Texas

1965

Helps pass the Voting Rights Act, which bans poll taxes

1960

1961

Soviet cosmonaut Yuri Gagarin is the first human to enter space

1963

Kenya becomes an independent republic with Jomo Kenyatta as its first president

1966

The National Organization for Women (NOW) is established to work for equality between women and men

GONZALEZ'S LIFE

1977

Becomes chair
of House
Assassinations
Committee

1981

Elected chairman
of the House
Subcommittee on
Housing and
Community
Development

1989

Elected chairman of
the House Banking,
Finance and Urban
Affairs Committee

1980

1986

The U.S. space
shuttle *Challenger*
explodes, killing all
seven astronauts
on board

1976

U.S. military
academies
admit women

WORLD EVENTS

1994

Earns Profile in Courage Award from the John F. Kennedy Library

1998

Chooses not to run for reelection to Congress because of health reasons

2000

Dies November 28 at Baptist Medical Center in San Antonio

2000

1994

Genocide of 500,000 to 1 million of the minority Tutsi group by rival Hutu people in Rwanda

2000

Draft of the human genome is completed

DATE OF BIRTH: May 3, 1916

BIRTHPLACE: San Antonio, Texas

FATHER: Leonides Gonzalez
(1875–1966)

MOTHER: Genoveva Barbosa
Gonzalez (1884–1975)

EDUCATION: San Antonio Junior
College and St. Mary's
University School of Law
in San Antonio, Texas

SPOUSE: Pura Berta "Bertha"
Cuellar Gonzalez
(c. 1920–)

DATE OF MARRIAGE: November 23, 1940

CHILDREN: Henry Jr. (1941–)
Rose Mary (1942–)
Charles (1945–)
Bertha (1947–)
Stephen (1951–)
Genevieve (1953–)
Frank (1954–)
Anna (1958–)

DATE OF DEATH: November 28, 2000

PLACE OF BURIAL: San Fernando Cemetery
II in San Antonio, Texas

In the Library

Adams, Simon, and David Hamilton Murdoch. *Texas.* New York: DK Children, 2003.

Flynn, Jean. *Henry B. Gonzalez: Rebel with a Cause.* Austin, Texas: Eakin Press, 2004.

Hoobler, Dorothy, and Thomas Hoobler. *The Mexican American Family Album.* New York: Oxford University Press, 1998.

Kanellos, Nicolas. *Hispanic Firsts: 500 Years of Extraordinary Achievement.* Detroit: Gale, 1997.

Netzley, Patricia D. *The Assassination of President John F. Kennedy.* New York: New Discovery Books, 1994.

Sloane, Todd A. *Gonzalez of Texas: A Congressman for the People.* Evanston, Ill.: John Gordon Burke, Inc., 1996.

Straub, Deborah Gillian. *Hispanic American Voices.* Detroit: UXL, 1997.

Look for more Signature Lives
books about this era:

Andrew Carnegie: *Captain of Industry*

Carrie Chapman Catt: *A Voice for Women*

J. Edgar Hoover: *Controversial FBI Director*

Langston Hughes: *The Voice of Harlem*

Douglas MacArthur: *America's General*

Eleanor Roosevelt: *First Lady of the World*

Elizabeth Cady Stanton: *Social Reformer*

On the Web

For more information on *Henry Gonzalez,* use FactHound to track down Web sites related to this book.

1. Go to *www.facthound.com*
2. Type in this book ID: 0756509963
3. Click on the *Fetch It* button.

FactHound will find the best Web sites for you.

Historic Sites

The Texas Capitol Building Visitors Center
112 E. 11th St.
Austin, TX 78711
512/305-8400
To visit the Texas Legislature, where Henry Gonzalez served as a senator

National Civil Rights Museum
450 Mulberry St.
Memphis, TN 38103
901/521-9699
To learn more about the movement to win basic rights for America's racial minorities

abject
being of the lowest or worst kind

antipathy
hate

colleagues
people with whom a person works

conspiracy
a plot involving more than one person

constituents
residents represented by an elected official

fraud
using deception to take something of value

gringo
a Latin American term for a non-Hispanic person

integrity
devotion to honesty and honor

liberal
in favor of political change and reform

pervasive
widespread

priorities
the ranking of how important things are

probation
close supervision of offenders instead of jail time

segregated
groups of people kept apart

tuberculosis
a lung disease causing fever, coughing, and
chest pain

Chapter 1

Page 9, line 13: "Henry B. Gonzalez." Contemporary Hispanic Biography. Vol. 2. Gale Group, 2002. Reproduced in Biography Resource Center. Farmington Hills, Mich.: Thomson Gale. 2004. http://galenet.galegroup.com/servlet/BioRC

Chapter 2

Page 17, line 4: Caroline Kennedy. *Profiles in Courage for Our Time.* New York: Hyperion, 2002, p. 95.

Page 23, 19: Ibid., p. 94

Page 24, line 13: Ibid., p. 95.

Page 25, line 4: Ibid., p. 96.

Chapter 3

Page 32, line 17: Jean Flynn. *Henry B. Gonzalez: Rebel with a Cause.* Austin, Texas: Eakin Press, 2004, p. 34.

Chapter 4

Page 36, line 1: Ibid., p. 39.

Page 36, line 27: Ibid., p. 42.

Page 38, line 14: *Profiles in Courage for Our Time*, p. 98.

Page 39, line 18: *Henry B. Gonzalez: Rebel with a Cause*, p. 43.

Page 41, line 1: Ibid., p. 45.

Chapter 5

Page 45, line 10: *Profiles in Courage for Our Time*, p. 99.

Page 45, line 22: Ibid., p. 99.

Page 46, line 5: *Henry B. Gonzalez: Rebel with a Cause*, p. 52.

Page 46, line 17: *Profiles in Courage for Our Time*, p. 99.

Page 47, line 1: *Henry B. Gonzalez: Rebel with a Cause*, p. 55.

Page 48, line 4: Ibid., p. 85.

Page 49, line 1: Ibid., p. 85:

Page 51, line 26: *Profiles in Courage for Our Time*, p. 100–101.

Page 52, line 16: Ibid., p. 101.

Chapter 6

Page 62, line 19: Josh Gottheimer. *Ripples of Hope: Great American Civil Rights Speeches.* New York: Basic Books, 2003, p. 331–332.

Page 63, line 2: Ibid., p. 332.

Page 63, line 5: Ibid., p. 332.

Page 63, line 12: Ibid., p. 332.

Page 64, line 8: *Henry B. Gonzalez: Rebel with a Cause*, p. 69.

Page 64, sidebar: Handbill from Henry B. Gonzalez bearing December 1888 quote from Henry Cabot Lodge, Pan-American Press—Rush Printers, San Antonio, Texas.

Page 65, line 1: *Profiles in Courage for Our Time*, p. 103.

Page 67, line 10: Ibid., p. 102.

Chapter 8

Page 78, line 4: *Henry B. Gonzalez: Rebel With a Cause*, p. 92.

Page 81, line 4: Bruce Davidson. "Henry B. Gonzalez rattles Capitol Hill." *San Antonio Express-News*, December 31, 1989.

Page 83, line 23: *Henry B. Gonzalez: Rebel with a Cause*, p. 104.

Chapter 9

Page 87, line 8: Kemper Diehl. "Gonzalez: Minorities Must 'Join Mainstream' to End 'Injustices.'" *San Antonio Express*, January 6, 1971.

Page 87, line 20: Ibid.

Page 88, line 5: Jim Eskin, *San Antonio Business Journal*, as quoted in Henry B. Gonzalez Foundation to Inspire Public Service pamphlet.

Page 89, line 6: *Henry B. Gonzalez: Rebel With a Cause*, p. 111.

Chapter 10

Page 91, line 10: *Profiles in Courage for Our Time*, p. 106.

Page 92, line 7: Washingtonpost.com. "Rep. Gonzalez to Retire at Year's End." September 5, 1997.

Page 92, line 11: Ibid.

Page 93, line 7: James E. Garcia. "Maverick Congressman Memorialized as 'A Voice for the Downtrodden.'" http://www.politicomagazine.com/henryb112900.html.

Page 94, line 4: Henry B. Gonzalez memorial card, November 2000.

Page 94, line 9: Ibid.

Page 94, line 17: Natalie Gott. "More than a thousand gather to mourn Henry B. Gonzalez." *Corpus Christi Caller Times*, December 3, 2000.

Page 94, line 26: "Henry B. Gonzalez." Contemporary Hispanic Biography. Vol. 2. Gale Group, 2002. Reproduced in Biography Resource Center. Farmington Hills, Mich.: Thomson Gale. 2004. http://galenet.galegroup.com/servlet/BioRC.

Page 95, line 9: *Henry B. Gonzalez: Rebel With a Cause*, p. 91.

Biographical Directory of the United States Congress, http://bioguide.congress.gov/scripts/biodisplay.pl?index=G000272.

Federal Deposit Insurance Corporation, http://www.fdic.gov/bank/historical/s&l/.

Gottheimer, Josh. *Ripples of Hope: Great American Civil Rights Speeches*. New York: Basic Books, 2003.

The History Channel, http://www.historychannel.com/speeches/archive/speech_403.html.

Kennedy, Caroline. *Profiles in Courage for Our Time*. New York: Hyperion, 2002.

Laezman, Rick. *100 Hispanic-Americans Who Shaped American History*. San Mateo, Calif.: Bluewood Books, 2002.

Library of Congress, http://www.loc.gov/rr/hispanic/congress/gonzalez.html.

Meyer, Nicholas E. *Biographical Dictionary of Hispanic Americans*. New York: Checkmark Books, 2001.

National Housing Institute, www.nhi.org/online/issues/98/pitcoff.htm.

The Washington Post, http://www.wpni.com/wp-srv/politics/campaigns/keyraces98/stories/txhouse090597.htm.

Brenda Haugen started in the newspaper business and had a career as an award-winning journalist before finding her niche as an author. Since then, she has written and edited many books, most of them for children. A graduate of the University of North Dakota in Grand Forks, Brenda lives in North Dakota with her family.

Image Credits